Gr 3-4

J
974.7
M          Mezzanotte, Jim
           New York


           *Wantagh Public Library*

# NEW YORK

by Jim Mezzanotte

GARETH**STEVENS**

**GS**

P U B L I S H I N G

A Member of the WRC Media Family of Companies

Please visit our web site at: www.garethstevens.com
For a free color catalog describing Gareth Stevens Publishing's
list of high-quality books and multimedia programs, call
1-800-542-2595 (USA) or 1-800-387-3178 (Canada).
Gareth Stevens Publishing's fax: (414) 332-3567.

Library of Congress Cataloging-in-Publication Data

Mezzanotte, Jim.
    New York / Jim Mezzanotte.
        p. cm. — (Portraits of the states)
    Includes bibliographical references and index.
    ISBN 0-8368-4630-3 (lib. bdg.)
    ISBN 0-8368-4649-4 (softcover)
    1. New York (State)—Juvenile literature.  I. Title.  II. Series.
    F119.3.M46    2005
    974.7—dc22                                    2005042673

This edition first published in 2006 by
**Gareth Stevens Publishing**
A Member of the WRC Media Family of Companies
330 West Olive Street, Suite 100
Milwaukee, WI  53212  USA

This edition copyright © 2006 by Gareth Stevens, Inc.

Editorial direction:  Mark J. Sachner
Project manager:  Jonatha A. Brown
Editor:  Betsy Rasmussen
Art direction and design:  Tammy West
Picture research:  Diane Laska-Swanke
Indexer:  Walter Kronenberg
Production:  Jessica Morris and Robert Kraus

Picture credits:  Cover, pp. 4, 5, 21, 22, 26 © Corel; p. 6 © Kean Collection/
Getty Images; p. 10 © Lewis W. Hine/George Eastman House/Getty Images;
p. 12 © CORBIS; pp. 15, 27 © Melvin Levine/Time & Life Pictures/Getty Images;
p. 16 © Edwin Levick/Getty Images; pp. 24, 28 © Gibson Stock Photography;
p. 29 © Photo File/MLB Photos via Getty Images

Printed in the United States of America

1 2 3 4 5 6 7 8 9 09 08 07 06 05

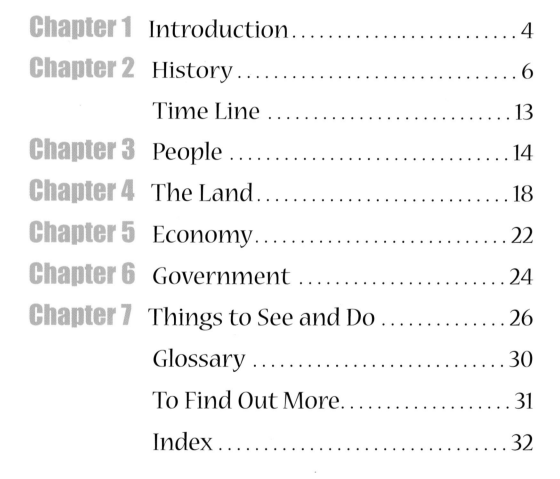

Words that are defined in the Glossary appear
in **bold** the first time they are used in the text.

On the Cover:  The Statue of Liberty has welcomed many people to the
United States.

# Introduction

**W**hat kind of place would you like to visit? A big, bustling city? A quiet farm? A sandy beach on the ocean? In the state of New York, you can visit all of these places.

The state is home to New York City, the largest city in the United States. This city is packed with tall buildings and millions of people.

But there is much more to New York than New York City. It also has farms and small towns. It has beautiful mountains, lakes, and forests. It has ocean beaches, too. People have come from many different countries to settle in New York. With all the different places and people, New York is many worlds in one!

**New York City has many buildings packed together. But it also has a big park, called Central Park.**

The state flag of New York.

# NEW YORK FACTS

- Became the 11th State:  July 26, 1788
- Population (2004):  19,227,088
- Capital:  Albany
- Biggest Cities:  New York City, Buffalo, Rochester, Yonkers
- Size:  47,214 square miles (122,284 square kilometers)
- Nickname:  The Empire State
- State Tree:  Sugar maple
- State Flower:  Rose
- State Animal:  Beaver
- State Bird:  Eastern bluebird

# History

Native Americans first settled in New York thousands of years ago. They farmed the rich soil in river valleys. For many years, different tribes fought each other. In the 1500s, some of these tribes joined together in a group. They formed the Iroquois Confederacy. They mostly stopped fighting each other.

### New Arrivals

Giovanni da Verrazano was probably the first European in New York. He sailed into New York Harbor in 1524 and explored the area for France. In 1609, Henry Hudson came. He worked for Britain. He and his crew sailed up the Hudson River. It is named after him.

Henry Hudson and his men meet Native Americans. They are sailing on the river that is named after him.

Later, the Dutch settled on this river. They farmed and traded furs with the Natives. They called the area New Netherland. In 1624, they built their first lasting settlement. They named it

Fort Orange. They also built New Amsterdam, where the river met the ocean. It is said that Dutch governor Peter Minuit paid the Natives a small sum for the land of New Amsterdam.

## A Fight for Control

New Amsterdam kept growing. Many ships passed through its harbor. They brought goods to the British **colonies** along the Atlantic Coast.

### Steamboats

Steamboats changed how people and things traveled. Faster than sailing ships, steamboats did not need wind. Robert Fulton built some of the first steamboats. In 1809, his steamboat traveled on the Hudson River. It went from New York City to Albany in thirty-two hours. A sailing ship needed four days to make this trip!

The British wanted New Amsterdam. In 1664, they sent ships to the city. Dutch governor Peter Stuyvesant surrendered the city. The British changed the city's name to New York. Fort Orange became Albany. The whole area was now called New York.

From 1754 to 1763, the French and British fought the French and Indian War. Native tribes also fought in this war. Some battles took place in New York. In 1763, the British won the war.

## Revolutionary War

By the 1770s, New York was a British colony, and it was ruled by people in Britain. At the time, many colonists did not want British rule, so they fought a war to win independence.

The Revolutionary War began in 1775. American colonists fought British troops. Many important battles were fought in New York. British troops held New York City for most of the war, but the Americans won the Battle of Saratoga. This battle proved to European countries that the colonies could beat the British. In 1783, Britain lost. The colonies became the United States. In 1788, New York became the eleventh state to join the United States. New York City was the first U.S. capital.

## Full Steam Ahead

In the 1800s, New York went through many changes. More people settled there. By 1820, it had more people than any other state. In 1825, workers finished the Erie Canal. It connected Lake Erie and the Hudson

### IN NEW YORK'S HISTORY

**A Dark Past**

After the Revolutionary War, many people lived well in New York, but other people did not. Some Native tribes helped the British during the Revolutionary War. American soldiers destroyed their villages to punish them. New York also had slaves from Africa. The state did not free all its slaves until the 1820s.

River. **Steamboats** could now travel through New York from the Great Lakes to the Atlantic Ocean. By the 1830s, railroads had been built, too.

New York became a big center for business. **Factories** were built. Many **immigrants** arrived in the state. They came from other countries. Many worked in the state's factories.

In 1861, the Civil War began. Southern states wanted to keep slavery. Northern states wanted to end it. Southern states left the Union. They formed their own country called the Confederate States of America. They fought against Northern states. Some people in New York did not want to fight in the war. They started riots in

## IN NEW YORK'S HISTORY

### Women's Rights

In 1848, a group of women met in Seneca Falls, New York. They talked about ways to improve women's rights. At the time, women had fewer rights than men. They could not even vote! The meeting was a first step for more women's rights.

**Immigrants sew clothes in 1905. They are in a New York City apartment. Back then, many immigrants worked in small, crowded places.**

New York City. But many New Yorkers fought in Civil War battles. In 1865, the North won. Southern states rejoined the Union.

## The Twentieth Century

In the early 1900s, businesses kept growing. Immigrants continued to arrive in New York City. The city had many poor people. They often lived and worked in awful conditions.

In the 1930s, the **Great**

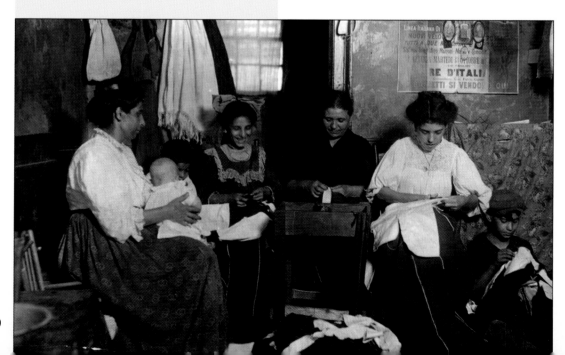

### A Tragic Fire

In 1911, a fire broke out in the Triangle Shirtwaist Factory in New York City. The fire killed 146 people, mostly women and girls. These workers had been locked inside the factory. They could not get out in time. After the fire, new laws were passed. The laws helped improve conditions for workers in the United States.

were built. The St. Lawrence Seaway was built so that large ships could travel inland. Big ships still use it today.

## Famous People of New York

# Franklin Delano Roosevelt

**Born:** January 30, 1882, Hyde Park, New York

**Died:** April 12, 1945, Warm Springs, Georgia

Franklin Delano Roosevelt was U.S. president from 1933 to 1945. He is the only president elected four times. Roosevelt was president during the Great Depression and World War II. He helped create jobs and make life better for many Americans. Franklin was not the first Roosevelt to be U.S. president. Theodore Roosevelt became president in 1901. He was from New York, too.

**Depression** began. During this time, millions of workers lost their jobs. In 1941 the United States entered World War II. Many U.S. soldiers went to fight in Europe. The state helped make planes, weapons, and other things needed for the war. Its **economy** improved.

After the war, the economy kept getting better. New bridges and highways

New York City was chosen as the home for the **United Nations**, or UN. Most of the world's countries belong to the UN. It works to keep peace among nations.

**Manhattan is famous for its many tall buildings.**

### September 11 Attacks

On September 11, 2001, terrorists attacked in New York City. They flew planes into two towers of the World Trade Center. Each tower was a building more than one hundred stories tall. The buildings fell, and about three thousand people died.

People in the city and throughout the world were shocked and saddened by this tragedy. Within a few years, the city had bounced back, and it began to put up new buildings at the World Trade Center site.

### New York Today

New York is still improving. It is trying to fix problems it has. Immigrants still come to New York City.

| | |
|---|---|
| **1524** | Italian Giovanni da Verrazzano explores part of state. |
| **1609** | Henry Hudson explores New York. |
| **1625** | The Dutch settle New Amsterdam, which later becomes New York City. |
| **1664** | The British take over control of New York. |
| **1775–1783** | The Revolutionary War is fought. |
| **1788** | New York becomes the eleventh state. |
| **1809** | Robert Fulton's steamboat travels from New York City to Albany. |
| **1848** | Seneca Falls Convention is held to discuss women's rights. |
| **1892–1924** | Twenty-two million immigrants pass through Ellis Island in New York Harbor. |
| **1949** | New York City becomes home to the United Nations headquarters. |
| **1959** | The St. Lawrence Seaway opens. |
| **2000** | Hillary Rodham Clinton is elected U.S. senator from New York. |
| **2001** | Terrorists use planes to attack the World Trade Center. Thousands of people are killed or injured. |
| **2004** | The Republican presidential convention is held in New York City. |

# People

New York is home to more than nineteen million people. Only two other states have more people. New York's population is still growing.

While some New Yorkers live on farms or in small towns, most live in cities and suburbs. New York City is the largest city in the state, and it is the largest in the entire country. More than eight million people live there. In fact, it has more people than most states!

**Hispanics:** In the 2000 U.S. Census, 15.1 percent of the people in the state of New York called themselves Latino or Hispanic. Most of them or their relatives came from places where Spanish is spoken. They may come from different racial backgrounds.

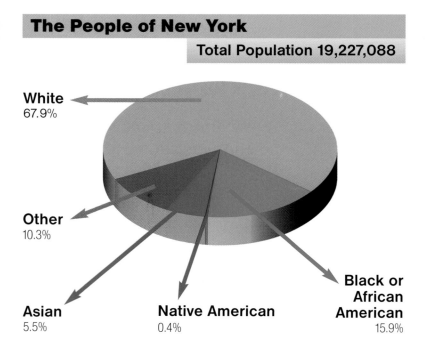

**The People of New York**

Total Population 19,227,088

White 67.9%

Other 10.3%

Asian 5.5%

Native American 0.4%

Black or African American 15.9%

Percentages are based on 2000 Census.

This building is on Ellis Island. Many immigrants passed through it when they came to America.

## Many People, Many Cultures

Years ago, Native Americans were the only people in New York. Then, people arrived from Europe and other places. They farmed and traded furs with Native Americans. Later, more people came. They helped build the Erie Canal, and they helped build railroads. They worked in the state's factories, too.

By the late 1800s, New York had many immigrants. Thousands arrived in New York City every day. Some went to live in other places, but many stayed in the city. Immigrants first stopped at Ellis Island, which is in New York Harbor. At Ellis Island, they went to a special center. After officials checked them, they entered the country.

**Immigrants come into New York Harbor in 1915. They are seeing the Statue of Liberty for the first time.**

15 percent of New Yorkers are African American. Very few Native Americans now live in New York.

New York City has people of many races and **cultures**. Sometimes people of one culture live together in their own communities. In some of these neighborhoods, you can find signs that are printed in a language other than English. Sometimes, different cultures mix together. Over the years as cultures have mixed, new traditions have been created. An important part of culture is food. In New York City, every kind of food is available.

This center was open from 1892 to 1954. More than twelve million people passed through Ellis Island during that time, although most of them came through between 1892 and 1924.

Today, fewer immigrants come from Europe. Instead, many come from Asia and Latin America. More than

## Religion and Education

More than 60 percent of New Yorkers are Christians. Most of them are Catholics. Almost 10 percent of New Yorkers are Jewish. Other people in the state are Muslims, Hindus, and Buddhists.

New York has many colleges and universities. The oldest is Columbia University in New York City. When it opened in 1754, New York was still a British colony. Today, the school is one of the country's top schools. New York has a state university system, too. This system has campuses in many cities. Other top schools include Cornell University and New York University. The state is also home to the U.S. Military Academy at West Point. It trains officers for the army.

# Famous People of New York

# Kate Mullany

**Born:** About 1845, Ireland

**Died:** About 1906, Troy, New York

Kate Mullany was an immigrant from Ireland. She was also one of the first women to fight for fair working conditions. When she was nineteen, she worked in a laundry to support her mother and siblings. The hours at the laundry were long, and the pay was low. Also, this work could be dangerous. The water used was boiling hot, chemicals were used, and irons caused many burns. She decided to organize a union. She and two hundred other women successfully held a strike and gained a pay raise. The union Mullany formed lasted for five years, at a time when most only lasted a few months.

# The Land

New York has many mountains. They are very old but not very high. The state's highest point is Mt. Marcy. It is in the Adirondack Mountains, which are in the north of the state. It is 5,344 feet (1,629 meters) above sea level. The Catskill Mountains are in southern New York. Parts of New York, especially near the Great Lakes, are flat.

## Climate

New York's seasons have different types of weather. Winters in New York can be quite cold. Northern parts of the state get colder and have more snow than southern parts. In New York, springs are rainy, summers warm, and autumn cool.

## Beaches, Rivers, and Lakes

New York's ocean coastline is in the southeast corner of the state. In this corner, Long Island sticks into the Atlantic Ocean. It has miles of sandy beaches. New York Harbor is just west of Long Island. Ships can easily reach this harbor. It is a big reason why New York City became so important.

# NEW YORK

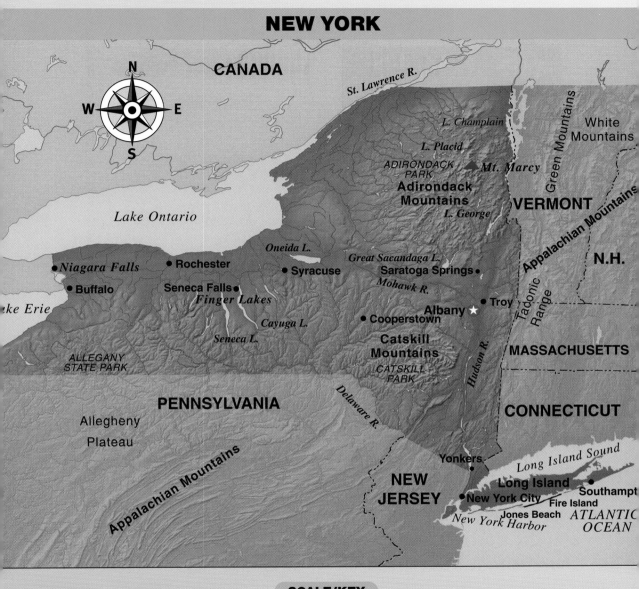

CANADA

*St. Lawrence R.*

*L. Champlain*

*L. Placid*

ADIRONDACK
PARK

▲ *Mt. Marcy*

**Adirondack
Mountains**

*L. George*

Green Mountains

White
Mountains

**VERMONT**

**N.H.**

*Lake Ontario*

*Oneida L.*

*Great Sacandaga L.*

● **Rochester**

*ke Erie*

● *Niagara Falls*

● **Buffalo**

**Seneca Falls**●

*Finger Lakes*

● **Syracuse**

**Saratoga Springs**●

*Mohawk R.*

● **Troy**

Appalachian Mountains

Tadonic Range

*Cayuga L.*

*Seneca L.*

ALLEGANY
STATE PARK

**Albany** ★

● **Cooperstown**

**Catskill
Mountains**

*CATSKILL
PARK*

*Hudson R.*

**MASSACHUSETTS**

**PENNSYLVANIA**

Allegheny

Plateau

*Delaware R.*

Appalachian Mountains

**CONNECTICUT**

**Yonkers**●

*Long Island Sound*

**Long Island**

**NEW
JERSEY**

●**New York City**

● **Southampt**

*Fire Island*

**Jones Beach**

*New York Harbor*

*ATLANTIC
OCEAN*

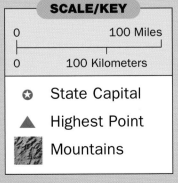

19

## Big Snow

Some parts of New York get huge amounts of snow. The cities of Buffalo, Rochester, and Syracuse get more snow than most other U.S. cities. They are in the northwest part of the state, along Lake Erie and Lake Ontario. Cold air flows over the lakes and dumps snow on the southern shores.

### Major Rivers

**Hudson River**
306 miles (492 km) long

**Delaware River**
280 miles (451 km) long

**Mohawk River**
148 miles (238 km) long

Two of the five Great Lakes form part of New York's border. Lake Erie is to the west, and Lake Ontario is to the north. Lake Champlain forms part of New York's eastern border. It connects to the Saint Lawrence Seaway. New York has more than eight thousand lakes inside its borders, too! The Finger Lakes are quite narrow.

The Hudson River is the state's longest river. Over the years, many ships used the Hudson River to carry goods. Other big rivers include the Delaware and Mohawk Rivers.

The St. Lawrence River forms part of New York's northern border. It is part of the St. Lawrence Seaway. Some rivers in the state have waterfalls. Niagara Falls is the most famous one.

## Plants and Animals

Forests cover more than half of New York. Trees in the

**Many people think Niagara Falls is an amazing sight!**

state include maple, oak, birch, and evergreens such as pine.

White-tailed deer are found all over New York. Black bears live in the Adirondack Mountains. Beavers, foxes, coyotes, and other small animals also live in New York. The state has more than three hundred species of birds. It has almost five hundred species of fish.

**Protecting the Environment**

New York has plenty of garbage and **pollution**.

Towns and cities in New York keep growing. They are taking over places that were once natural areas.

The state is trying to keep its land and water clean. It has passed laws to protect plants and animals and the places where they live. New York now has protected places for them to live.

## FUN FACTS

### Niagara Falls

Niagara Falls is on the Niagara River — on the western border of the United States and Canada. Each year, millions of people come to see the falls. It is one of the seven natural wonders of the world! At the falls, water drops 282 feet (86 m). More than 6 million cubic feet (169,800 cubic meters) of water go over the falls each second.

# Economy

New York has fewer factories than it once did, but they still provide jobs. Some factories print reading materials, such as books and magazines. Others make scientific instruments, equipment, and clothing. Many New Yorkers have service jobs. They do work that helps people. This work includes jobs in restaurants, hotels, and hospitals.

### Jobs in New York City

New York City is home to Wall Street, a world center for **finance**. Some people work at the New York Stock Exchange and the American Stock Exchange. They

These people work at the New York Stock Exchange. They buy and sell shares of companies.

buy and sell shares of stocks in companies. By owning a share of stock, you own a piece of a company. Other people have jobs in banking, insurance, and real estate. People also work in music, television, and publishing. Tourism is important to the New York economy, too. People from all over the world visit New York. Hotels, restaurants, and parks all need workers.

## Transportation and Farming

Transportation also provides jobs. New York has many airports and highways. John F. Kennedy airport is one of the largest and busiest in the world. New York has trains and ferries, too. Many ships dock at the Port of New York.

New York has many dairy farms. The state is known for its apples, grapes, corn, cherries, and hay, too.

## How Money Is Made in New York

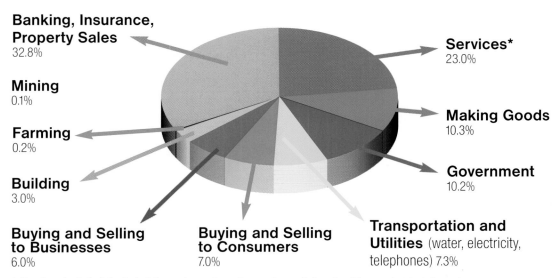

Banking, Insurance, Property Sales
32.8%

Mining
0.1%

Farming
0.2%

Building
3.0%

Buying and Selling to Businesses
6.0%

Buying and Selling to Consumers
7.0%

Transportation and Utilities (water, electricity, telephones) 7.3%

Services*
23.0%

Making Goods
10.3%

Government
10.2%

* Services include jobs in hotels, restaurants, auto repair, medicine, teaching, and entertainment.

# Government

Albany is the capital of New York. Lawmakers in the state work there. The state government has three parts, or branches. They are the executive, legislative, and judicial branches.

### Executive Branch

The executive branch carries out the state's laws and is headed by the governor. The lieutenant governor and other officials help the governor.

### Legislative Branch

New York's legislature has two parts,

New York's capitol building is in Albany. Workers began building it in 1867. They did not finish until 1899!

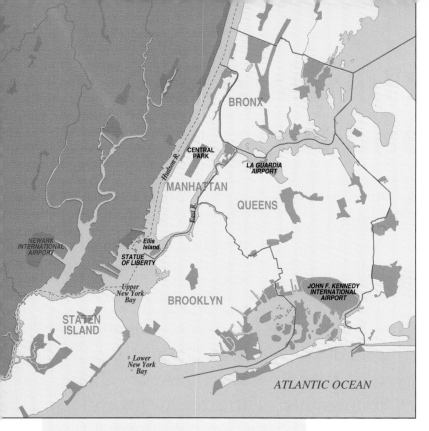

Labels on map: BRONX, CENTRAL PARK, LA GUARDIA AIRPORT, MANHATTAN, QUEENS, Hudson R., East R., NEWARK INTERNATIONAL AIRPORT, Ellis Island, STATUE OF LIBERTY, Upper New York Bay, BROOKLYN, JOHN F. KENNEDY INTERNATIONAL AIRPORT, STATEN ISLAND, Lower New York Bay, ATLANTIC OCEAN

## Judicial Branch

Judges and courts make up the judicial branch. Judges and courts may decide whether people who have been accused of committing crimes are guilty.

**There are five counties, or boroughs, that make up the city of New York. They are Staten Island, Brooklyn, Manhattan, Queens, and the Bronx.**

## Local Government

New York is divided into sixty-two counties. A group of people called a board of supervisors runs each county. New York has 62 cities and 932 towns. Most are led by a mayor.

called the senate and the assembly. The two work together to make state laws.

# NEW YORK'S STATE GOVERNMENT

| Executive | | Legislative | | Judicial | |
|---|---|---|---|---|---|
| **Office** | **Length of Term** | **Body** | **Length of Term** | **Court** | **Length of Term** |
| Governor | 4 years | Senate (62 members) | 2 years | Appeals | |
| Lieutenant Governor | 4 years | Assembly | | (7 Justices) | 14 years |
| | | (150 members) | 2 years | Appellate Court (48) | 5 years |

# Things to See and Do

New York City has museums for art and science. It has places to enjoy music, ballet, and opera. On a famous street called Broadway, people see musicals and other plays.

Many **tourists** visit two small islands in New York Harbor. One is Ellis Island. It has a museum about immigrants. The other is Liberty Island. It is home to the Statue of Liberty. This statue has welcomed many immigrants to their new country.

Time Square is in the center of Manhattan. It has many theaters. It is a colorful, exciting place!

# Colin Powell

**Born:** April 5, 1937, New York City, New York

Colin Powell grew up in New York City. He is the son of Jamaican immigrants. In 1989, he became chairman of the Joint Chiefs of Staff. Powell is the first African American to hold this position — the highest one in the U.S. military. From 2001 to 2005, Powell was U.S. Secretary of State. He is the first African American to hold this position, too.

## Outside New York City

Saratoga Springs is near Albany. People go there to enjoy music and dance in the summer. It also has a famous horse racing track. Farther west is Cooperstown. It is home to the National Baseball Hall of Fame.

Many tourists visit Niagara Falls, near Buffalo.

People enjoy the outdoors in New York. They visit the state's lakes and ocean beaches. Some go to Long

**Liberty Island, with Ellis Island behind it.**

## Famous People of New York

### Hillary Rodham Clinton

**Born:** October 26, 1947, Chicago, Illinois

Hillary Rodham Clinton is married to Bill Clinton, a former U.S. president. She was First Lady from 1993 to 2001. In 1999, the Clintons bought a house in New York. The next year, she was elected to be a U.S. senator from New York. Before Hillary Rodham Clinton, no First Lady had ever been elected to the Senate.

Island. Others go to the Finger Lakes. People also hike in the state's forests and mountains.

## Sports

New York has many professional sports teams. Its two baseball teams are the New York Yankees and the New York Mets. The Yankees have won the World Series more than twenty-five times. The state's football teams are the Buffalo Bills,

**This river is in the Finger Lakes region, near Ithaca.**

the New York Jets, and the New York Giants. The New York Knicks play in the National Basketball Association. The women's WNBA basketball team is called the New York Liberty. New York's hockey teams are the New York Islanders, the New York Rangers, and the Buffalo Sabres.

Soccer fans cheer for the New York Power.

From 1947 to 1956, Jackie Robinson played for the Brooklyn Dodgers.

### FUN FACTS

### The Brooklyn Dodgers

The Dodgers baseball team is in Los Angeles, California. But the team used to be in Brooklyn, a part of New York City. In 1947, the Dodgers made history. That year, Jackie Robinson joined the team. He was the first African American to play major league baseball.

**assassinated** — killed on purpose after planning

**colonies** — groups of people living in a new land but being controlled by the place they came from

**cultures** — the ways of life for certain countries or groups of people, including their history, art, and customs

**economy** — the making and using of goods and services

**factories** — buildings where goods and products are made

**finance** — having to do with buying and selling companies and lending them money

**Great Depression** — a time, in the 1930s, when many people lost their jobs and businesses lost money.

**immigrants** — people who come from one country to live in another country

**pollution** — waste that makes water or air unclean

**restored** — made to look new again

**steamboats** — boats that use steam from heated water for their power

**tourists** — people who travel for pleasure

**United Nations** — a group made up of many nations, which works for world peace

## Books

*E Is for Empire:  A New York Alphabet.*  Discover America State by State (series).  Ann Burg  (Thomson Gale)

*Franklin D. Roosevelt.*  Rookie Biographies (series).  Wil Mara  (Children's Press)

*New York.*  Rookie Read-About Geography (series).  Sarah De Capua  (Children's Press)

*New York Facts and Symbols.*  The States and Their Symbols (series).  Emily McAuliffe  (Bridgestone Books)

*New York, New York!  The Big Apple from A to Z.*  Laura Krauss Melmed  (HarperCollins)

*The Statue of Liberty.*  Places in American History (series).  Susan Ashley  (Weekly Reader Early Learning Library)

*Teddy Roosevelt:  The People's President.*  Stories of Famous Americans (series).  Sharon Gayle  (Aladdin Library)

## Web Sites

Enchanted Learning:  New York
www.enchantedlearning.com/usa/states/newyork

Facts about Niagara Falls
www.niagarafallslive.com/Facts_about_Niagara_Falls.htm